CW00692809

Original title:
Finding Myself Again

Author: Lan Donne
ISBN HARDBACK: 978-9916-89-835-2
ISBN PAPERBACK: 978-9916-89-836-9
ISBN EBOOK: 978-9916-89-837-6

Psalms of the Rediscovered Heart

In shadows deep, my spirit yearns,
A whisper stirs, where hope returns.
The light within begins to bloom,
Dispelling doubt, dispelling gloom.

In ancient words, my soul finds peace,
A melody that will not cease.
With every tear, a cleansing rain,
In joyous light, I break the chain.

The Covenant of Self-Renewal

In quiet moments, I reflect,
A promise made, my life to direct.
With open heart and open mind,
In every breath, my truth I find.

The storms may rage, the winds may howl,
Yet in my core, a sacred owl.
It guides my path, through thick and thin,
In self-renewal, I begin.

Introspection as Prayer

I turn within, my fervent plea,
In stillness, Lord, please speak to me.
Each thought a prayer, each sigh a song,
In this quiet space, I feel I belong.

The past may weigh, yet I release,
With every breath, I find my peace.
In introspection, grace unfolds,
In sacred whispers, love retold.

Seeking the Sacred Flame

O flame divine, within me glow,
Illuminate the path I know.
Through trials faced and lessons learned,
In every heart, Your love has burned.

With open hands, I seek Your grace,
In every smile, in every face.
For in the darkness, You remain,
My guiding star, my sacred flame.

Solace in the Presence

In the stillness, I find grace,
Wrapped in love, lost in space.
Holy whispers fill the air,
Comfort weaving everywhere.

In the shadow, faith does bloom,
Casting out all doubt and gloom.
Peace descends like gentle rain,
Washing over every pain.

Hearts uplifted, spirits soar,
Finding strength forevermore.
In this haven, I abide,
With the sacred at my side.

Celestial Reflections

Stars above in a velvet night,
Guiding souls with their soft light.
Each twinkle speaks a sacred truth,
Of hope restored and eternal youth.

Clouds drift like thoughts in the mind,
Unraveling mysteries, wondrously entwined.
In silence, I seek divine signs,
Where heaven and earth intertwines.

Mirrors of the soul's deep quest,
In the cosmos, we find our rest.
With every heartbeat, I reflect,
On the universe, deeply connected.

The Sacred Dance of Renewal

With every dawn, new life is born,
A sacred dance, the spirit's scorn.
In the rhythm of breath, we grow,
Fields of grace in radiant flow.

Steps of joy on hallowed ground,
Harmony in each sound.
Circles formed by love's embrace,
Lost and found in a holy space.

With each turn of seasons' wheel,
Hearts awaken to the real.
In the cycle, we are one,
Under the gaze of the nurturing sun.

Chant of the Wandering Spirit

Beyond the mountains, my heart does roam,
In search of truth, I make my home.
Each step unfolds a tale untold,
Of ancient wisdom, brave and bold.

Through valleys deep and rivers wide,
The spirit flows, it cannot hide.
With every whisper from the trees,
I find my path, my soul's degrees.

In the echoes, I hear the call,
Of love that binds us, one and all.
As I wander, I am free,
A child of earth, of sky, of sea.

Enkindled by the Flame Within

In silence deep, a fire glows,
A spark of light, where pure love flows.
It beckons gently, warms the heart,
A sacred dance where souls impart.

Through trials faced, the flame will rise,
Illuminating with hopeful sighs.
In darkest nights, let courage lead,
For in the flame, we find our creed.

The spirit sings, ignited bright,
A beacon shining through the night.
With every breath, the flame expands,
Uniting all in loving hands.

Let faith ignite the path we tread,
Awareness blooms where thoughts are fed.
Embrace the heat, the warmth within,
For through this flame, true life begins.

Awaken now, your heart's desire,
Let passion flow, let souls conspire.
In union strong, we find our place,
The flame within, our saving grace.

Seeds of Sacred Awareness

In fertile ground, a seed is sown,
With prayerful whispers, it has grown.
A bud of wisdom, gently breaks,
Awakening joy, the spirit wakes.

The sunlight bathes each tender shoot,
In vibrant hues, the truth takes root.
With every breath, the world expands,
In sacred trust, we join our hands.

When doubts arise, let courage call,
The seeds we plant will never fall.
For in the soil of love and grace,
Eternal blooms, we here embrace.

Each grain of faith, a story told,
In unity, our hearts unfold.
Together strong, we rise and sow,
The sacred seeds that help us grow.

So tend with care this precious earth,
Embrace the light, rejoice in birth.
For every seed, a promise bright,
With sacred love, we share the light.

The Harmony of the Inner Self

Within the quiet, peace will sing,
A melody that pulls the string.
Each note a prayer, a softly hum,
In rhythms pure, our hearts become.

The stillness wraps, a gentle shroud,
In unity, we feel so proud.
The harmony that dwells inside,
A sacred place where love abides.

In every thought, a pulse divine,
Connecting us as stars align.
With every breath, we feel the flow,
The rhythm of a love we know.

Through storms that rage and trials vast,
The inner self shall hold us fast.
With trust and faith, we rise anew,
In harmony, our spirits true.

So dance, dear soul, with grace and light,
Embrace the journey, take your flight.
For in the heart, where peace is found,
The harmony of life is crowned.

Whispers of the Celestial Soul

In twilight's glow, a whisper calls,
The soul's soft voice through nature sprawls.
An echo sweet, a gentle breeze,
Inviting hearts to find their peace.

The stars above, they shine and weave,
In patterns grand, we learn to believe.
Each cosmic thread, a story spun,
In harmony, we are made one.

With every heartbeat, let love soar,
In sacred silence, we explore.
The whispers guide us on our way,
Illuminating night and day.

In every glance, the universe,
A dance of light, a holy verse.
With open hearts, let spirit reign,
For in the whispers, there's no pain.

So heed the calls, the gentle sighs,
For in their grace, our truth implies.
The celestial soul, a wondrous sight,
In whispers sweet, we find our light.

The Embrace of Graceful Healing

In shadows deep, where sorrows lie,
A gentle hand lifts hearts on high.
With whispered prayers, the spirit mends,
In grace, the broken soul descends.

In every tear, a blessing flows,
A sacred touch, the journey grows.
Faith blooms bright in darkened hours,
Through trials faced, the soul empowers.

The sun will rise on weary nights,
With hope restored, the heart ignites.
In quiet moments, peace shall reign,
Through love and light, we break the chain.

So trust the path that leads us home,
For in His grace, we are not alone.
Together we stand, in joy or strife,
Embraced by healing, blessed with life.

Let burdens lift, let spirits soar,
In unity, our hearts explore.
Each step forward, a sacred call,
The embrace of grace shall heal us all.

Celestial Reflections

Beneath the stars, where dreams ignite,
We search for truth in sacred light.
Each twinkle shines a guiding way,
To lead us through the darkest day.

With every breath, the cosmos sings,
In harmony, creation clings.
The night unveils divine designs,
In whispered tales, the heart entwines.

A mirror held to souls so pure,
Reflects the love that will endure.
From galaxies to the fragile seed,
In every flower, we find our creed.

Let silence guide our minds to see,
The beauty found in mystery.
In stillness, we embrace the vast,
Celestial wonders, unsurpassed.

So travel forth, in peace reside,
With stars above, our faith the guide.
In every light, a spark revealed,
In cosmic grace, our hearts are healed.

The Temple of Rediscovery

Within the walls where echoes dwell,
Awakened souls begin to tell.
The stories lost through years gone by,
In every whisper, the truths reply.

A sacred space for hearts to mend,
In quiet corners, we make amends.
With open arms, the past is met,
In love's embrace, no more regret.

The lessons learned so deeply sown,
In every heart, a seed is grown.
Through trials faced, and shadows fled,
The temple rises where faith is fed.

With every step, our spirits dance,
In moments pure, we take a chance.
Rediscovering the light within,
In every loss, there's hope to begin.

So gather near, in love we find,
The sacred bond that intertwines.
In unity, we break the chains,
The temple stands, where love remains.

Heartbeats in the Silence

In silent prayer, our spirits rise,
A gentle pulse, unseen, describes.
Each heartbeat echoes through the night,
In every pause, we find the light.

With whispered hopes and dreams untold,
The quiet strength begins to unfold.
In stillness true, we softly breathe,
In heartbeats shared, our souls believe.

In moments hushed, love speaks so clear,
A melody that draws us near.
In gentle rhythm, we unite,
Through silence deep, our hearts take flight.

So let us linger in this space,
Where grace abounds and time's embrace.
In every heartbeat, truth shall flow,
In silence, endless love will grow.

Together here, in peace we find,
The sacred bond that ties mankind.
With every heartbeat, we are one,
In silent joy, our journey's begun.

Awakening the Soul's Lantern

In the quiet dawn, a whisper calls,
The heart ignites, as darkness falls.
A flame retrieved from depths unknown,
Guiding steps to realms unshown.

With open arms, the spirit bends,
To trace the path where love transcends.
Each tear a spark, each sigh a prayer,
Illumined truth in sacred air.

Beneath the stars, the lantern sways,
A beacon bright for wandering days.
In every heart, a light shall rise,
Awakening hopes, to touch the skies.

Through trials faced and shadows cast,
The soul finds strength, its fears surpassed.
In unity, we stand, we seek,
The sacred flame, through voices meek.

Awake, arise, let courage soar,
Embrace the light forevermore.
In luminous grace, let hearts unite,
Awakening the soul's pure light.

The Pilgrim's Return

Upon the road, the pilgrim treads,
With weary feet and dreams unfed.
Through winding paths of joy and pain,
He seeks the place where love remains.

Each step he takes, the earth may sigh,
As whispered hopes ascend the sky.
In longing hearts, the echoes swell,
Of distant lands where spirits dwell.

With open eyes, he views the morn,
A world reborn, where peace is sworn.
In sacred silence, truth revealed,
A journey deep, a fate concealed.

At journey's end, the fire ignites,
An ember born of countless nights.
In every tear, a lesson learned,
The flame of faith forever burned.

Return from afar, with wisdom gained,
Through trials faced, and strength unchained.
In every soul, a story weaves,
The pilgrim's heart, as love believes.

Through the Veil of Shadows

In twilight's hush, the shadows play,
Where light and darkness softly sway.
The veil that thins, the truth unveiled,
A sacred dance where fear is quelled.

Within the night, the stars align,
To guide the lost, a path divine.
In gentle whispers, hope resounds,
Through every heart, salvation found.

Each tear a prayer, each sigh a song,
Through hidden realms where dreams belong.
The sacred space where souls collide,
In love's embrace, no need to hide.

Beyond the veil, the light breaks free,
In every heart, a mystery.
With courage found, we step anew,
Through shadows deep, the light shines true.

So take my hand, and we shall tread,
Where love and light, our spirits fed.
Together rise, for we are whole,
Transcending all, awakening soul.

Rebirth Amidst the Ashes

From embers cold, a spark ignites,
A phoenix born from winter's nights.
Through ashes deep, the soul ascends,
In sacred fire, the spirit mends.

With every tear that falls like rain,
The heart transforms from grief to gain.
In darkness faced, the light is drawn,
To greet the dawn, a new life's song.

Through trials borne, the strength unveils,
The beauty found in all that fails.
In every heart, a story told,
Of love's embrace, of faith's pure gold.

The past released, the future bright,
In every breath, a glimmered light.
With hope renewed, we rise again,
Rebirth amidst the sacred pain.

So let us dance, in joyous cries,
For from the ashes, our spirit flies.
In unity, our hearts proclaim,
The beauty found in love's great name.

A Seraph's Embrace

In the light where angels dwell,
A seraph sings, all is well.
Wings unfurled, a gentle touch,
In their arms, we feel so much.

Heaven's whispers, soft and pure,
Guiding hearts, our souls secure.
With each note, we rise and soar,
Finding peace forevermore.

Beneath their gaze, our fears dissolve,
In love's embrace, we all evolve.
Radiant beams of hope align,
In this realm, our spirits shine.

Lost in grace, we shun despair,
In sacred spaces, breathe the air.
With every heartbeat, we connect,
In seraph's light, we are perfect.

Together bound, through trials faced,
In union strong, we find our place.
For in the arms of angel kin,
The journey starts, let life begin.

Renewal in the Garden of Reflection

In gardens lush, green dreams await,
Where petals fall, never too late.
Through fragrant blooms, the soul takes flight,
In nature's arms, we find the light.

Reflecting still on waters clear,
Each ripple brings our thoughts more near.
With hands in soil, we plant the seeds,
Nurtured with love, our spirit feeds.

The sun arises, whispers grace,
Each dawn reveals a sacred space.
In every leaf, a story told,
Of prayers spoken, dreams of old.

As seasons change, the heart expands,
With gentle care, we hold His hands.
In quiet moments, we renew,
Our faith restored, our vision true.

Together here, we breathe anew,
In sacred gardens, love shines through.
With every breath, the world aligned,
In reflection's peace, our souls entwined.

The Journey Within

In silence deep, the spirit calls,
A journey starts, where wisdom falls.
Into the depths of heart and mind,
In sacred stillness, truth we find.

With every step, the path unfolds,
In shadows cast, the light beholds.
Through trials faced and doubts released,
Our inner strength, a whispered feast.

Each breath we take, a prayer, a song,
In solitude, we learn to belong.
Embracing warmth, the love inside,
In faith, we walk, we do not hide.

Through valleys low and mountains high,
We seek the stars in evening sky.
For in the darkness, there's a spark,
Leading us forth, igniting the dark.

In unity with all that's near,
The journey within, we hold dear.
For every heart's a sacred space,
In God we dwell, in love's embrace.

Sacred Traces of the Heart

Each heartbeat echoes sacred themes,
A silent vow, a tapestry of dreams.
In stitched together moments spent,
The traces form a life well lent.

With every tear, a lesson learned,
In flames of hope, the spirit burned.
Through trials faced, we rise again,
In love's embrace, we find our zen.

In whispers soft, the past remains,
Each joyful cry, each tender pain.
In sacred traces, we reflect,
On paths we've walked, the love we protect.

The heart's a canvas, paint it well,
With stories rich, where spirits dwell.
For life is art, a gift divine,
In every pulse, His love does shine.

With open arms, we greet the day,
In gratitude, our hearts will stay.
For every moment, a chance to start,
In sacred traces of the heart.

The Spirit's Quiet Revelation

In silence deep, the spirit sings,
A whisper soft, of sacred things.
The heart unfolds, with gentle grace,
In quietude, we seek His face.

The dawn breaks slow, a holy light,
Illuminates the path so right.
With every step, the truth shall grow,
In faith's embrace, our spirits flow.

Beneath the stars, the night reveals,
The hidden truths that silence heals.
The breath of life, a sacred sigh,
In stillness found, we learn to fly.

With every tear, a lesson learned,
In every loss, our hearts have turned.
To seek the peace, within the strife,
To find the joy, within this life.

And so we walk, with hearts anew,
In every moment, He is true.
The Spirit guides, our souls align,
In quiet grace, the light will shine.

Echoes of a Forgotten Prayer

Upon the winds, a prayer takes flight,
A whispered hope, lost to the night.
In shadows deep, remembrance stirs,
The echoes call, through time's soft purrs.

Amidst the noise, we strain to hear,
The sacred words that draw us near.
In every sigh, a longing grows,
A bridge to grace, that softly flows.

In ancient texts, the echoes dwell,
A truth that time cannot repel.
In every heart, the ember glows,
Of faith reborn, as love bestows.

So let us pause, and heed the call,
In silence found, we shall not fall.
Each prayer we've sent, they rise again,
In unity, we seek the pen.

For every tear, and every plea,
Is woven in the tapestry.
The echoes laced, in love's embrace,
Reveal the path to boundless grace.

The Pathway to Inner Grace

In quiet meadows, shadows play,
A path of peace, where hearts may stay.
With footsteps light, we tread the stones,
Upon this road, our spirit's homes.

With every breath, the world unfolds,
The gift of grace, in love retold.
A gentle hand, a soothing balm,
In trials faced, we find the calm.

Through valleys low, and mountains high,
With open hearts, we dare to fly.
The essence pure, of love divine,
Guides each soul toward the design.

With each sunrise, a chance reborn,
To walk in light, no longer worn.
The journey is, the soul's embrace,
In every heart, lies sacred space.

As rivers flow, and stars align,
We find the thread, the heart's design.
In every step, the truth we trace,
And follow on, the path of grace.

In Search of the Divine Whisper

In hushed retreats, we seek the sound,
A whisper soft, where truth is found.
In shadows cast, the light reveals,
The sacred notes, that spirit seals.

With every breath, a prayer takes form,
Amidst the chaos, it becomes warm.
A subtle nudge, a guiding hand,
In search of peace, we take our stand.

Where silence reigns, the heart can hear,
The hidden voice that's ever near.
In moments still, beneath the sky,
The divine breath invites us nigh.

With faith as light, we trace the lines,
Of wisdom shared in ancient signs.
In every doubt, a trust shall grow,
As whispers call, and hearts bestow.

So let us journey, side by side,
In quest of love, our faithful guide.
In search of truth, we find the bliss,
In every heart, the divine kiss.

Tracing Footprints in Faith

In the quiet dawn, shadows blend,
Footprints lead where angels send.
The path is narrow, yet it glows,
With every step, His mercy flows.

We walk with hope, hand in hand,
In sacred whispers, we understand.
Through trials faced, our spirits rise,
We find our strength in whispered sighs.

Beneath the stars, our prayers take flight,
Guided by the softest light.
Each step, a testament of grace,
In faith's embrace, we find our place.

The journey long, the heart sincere,
In every doubt, He draws us near.
As mountains shift, and rivers bend,
His love is sure, it will not end.

With every tear, we grow anew,
For in our struggles, He breaks through.
Tracing dreams, our spirits soar,
In faith, we seek forevermore.

A Sojourn Towards the Inner Light

In silence deep, the heart aligns,
A journey born in sacred signs.
Through valleys low and mountains high,
We seek the truth that cannot lie.

With every breath, the spirit yearns,
The flame within, it brightly burns.
In moments still, we feel His grace,
A loving hand in every place.

The road is winding, yet it leads,
To waters pure, to holy creeds.
Each step we take, a prayer above,
In questing souls, we find His love.

The world may dim, and shadows creep,
But in our hearts, His light will keep.
With faith as guide, we find our way,
In darkest nights, we greet the day.

Through trials faced, hope does ignite,
In every soul, the inner light.
Sojourn we must, together strong,
With love and faith, we all belong.

The Mirage of Forgotten Self

In the desert dry, we chase a dream,
Lost in the sands, as hard as it seems.
What once was clear, now fades away,
In quest for truth, we often stray.

The mirage beckons, an alluring sight,
Promises of joy, wrapped in the night.
Yet deeper still, the soul must seek,
In silence loud, it calls to the meek.

Who am I, in this endless race?
A fleeting shadow, a worn-out face.
Yet in the stillness, a voice arises,
"Remember, dear child, where true worth lies."

The layers peel; we shed the skin,
To find the love that lies within.
Each step, a journey back to grace,
In sacred reflection, we find our place.

From forgotten dreams, we brave the tide,
Embracing the light that will not hide.
In unity found, we heal and mend,
The true self awakened, the love we send.

The Unfolding of Grace

In morning's light, the world awakes,
Each breath a gift, each moment shapes.
With gentle hands, the heart unfolds,
Revealing stories yet untold.

In quiet prayer, our souls entwine,
A tapestry woven, rich and divine.
Through trials faced and burdens shared,
The weight of life, together bared.

In kindness given, grace abounds,
In laughter's echo, love surrounds.
Through every tear, a lesson learned,
In vulnerability, hearts are turned.

The path ahead may twist and wind,
Yet in the journey, peace we find.
For in the struggle, light's embrace,
Unfolds the beauty of His grace.

Together we rise, in faith we stand,
United in spirit, hand in hand.
The unfolding joy, our spirits trace,
In endless love, the guide of grace.

Navigating the Labyrinth of the Self

In the shadowed paths I tread,
Seeking wisdom from within.
Each turn reveals a truth unsaid,
A whisper of my soul's own kin.

The mirrors reflect my deepest fears,
Yet grace shines through the cracks.
With every step, the path clears,
A guide amidst the sacred tracks.

In silence, I confront my past,
The burdens that weigh my heart.
I learn that pain cannot outlast,
When love and hope play their part.

The echoes of the ages call,
Urging me to rise anew.
In the labyrinth, I find it all,
The sacred light that guides me through.

Out of the maze, I step with grace,
Transforming shadows into light.
With every breath, I find my place,
In the universe, shining bright.

Under the Wing of the Holy

Beneath the vastness of the sky,
Where peace and solace reign.
I find my refuge, humbled, nigh,
The Holy One, my sacred gain.

The wind carries whispers soft,
As I seek to mend my soul.
In faith, I rise, like wings aloft,
Guided by love, made whole.

In every heart, a gentle spark,
A divine presence does reside.
Awakening light within the dark,
Inviting all to confide.

With open arms, I share my prayer,
In the stillness, I take flight.
Wrapped in love, I have no care,
For I am bathed in holy light.

Beneath the wing, I find my rest,
Surrendered to the love divine.
In this sacred space, I'm blessed,
Forever in the grace, I shine.

The Sacred Tapestry of Being

Threads of life interwoven tight,
A tapestry of love and grace.
Each color sings a truth, so bright,
In the Sacred One's embrace.

Moments woven into time,
In trials, joy and sorrow blend.
Every heartbeat, every rhyme,
A story, waiting to transcend.

In the patterns, a divine design,
Revealing purpose in the fray.
Each soul's journey, a sacred line,
Guides us on our destined way.

As we tread on paths unknown,
We're threads pulled from the same loom.
In every joy and pain we've sown,
We weave our hearts, dispelling gloom.

Together, we create the whole,
In unity, we shall arise.
For in each fiber lies the soul,
Reflected in the endless skies.

Embracing the Unseen

In silence, the unseen is revealed,
A presence felt, yet out of sight.
In the stillness, burdens healed,
I gather strength, igniting light.

The whispers of the divine call me,
In shadows, I uncover grace.
Embracing all that cannot be,
I find the sacred in this space.

With faith, I explore the unknown,
Guided by love's gentle hand.
In darkness, seeds of hope are sown,
As I learn to understand.

Each moment a precious gift,
Inviting me to trust the flow.
As I embrace, my spirits lift,
In the unseen, I come to know.

Together with the quiet night,
I walk the path unafraid.
In the unseen, I find my light,
A journey sacredly portrayed.

Angels of the Forgotten Journey

Angels whisper, soft and kind,
Guiding lost souls, the blind.
Through shadows deep, on paths untold,
They carry hope, like threads of gold.

With wings that shimmer, they take flight,
In the stillness of the night.
They watch over each weary heart,
A sacred bond, we're never apart.

In valleys low, where sorrow dwells,
Their gentle laughter breaks the shells.
Through trials fierce, they stand with grace,
Revealing light in every place.

When silence falls, and faith seems lost,
They gather near, no matter the cost.
An echo of love, eternally bright,
Angels embrace us, in holy light.

So hold your head, lift up your gaze,
For light will break through darkest haze.
In forgotten places, they reside,
Angels of hope, forever our guide.

The Revelation of Quietude

In stillness, the soul finds peace,
A gentle sigh, a sweet release.
The world fades away, soft and low,
In quietude, love starts to grow.

Whispers of grace in the morning light,
A sacred promise, ever bright.
Nature sings its soothing song,
In every heart, where we belong.

Beneath the trees, we pause and breathe,
The spirit's dance, the webs we weave.
Here, in silence, we find our way,
A journey shared, come what may.

Moments cherished, treasured still,
A sacred space, a loved one's will.
In revelation, truths unfold,
Quietude's warmth, a balm for the cold.

Take a step, embrace the calm,
In every heart, yield to the psalm.
With open arms and gentle hearts,
We find the grace in silence that imparts.

The Lattice of Spiritual Rebirth

In the garden, new life blooms,
From tangled roots and ancient tombs.
A lattice formed by faith's embrace,
This tapestry of divine grace.

Each thistle pricked, each tear that fell,
A story told, a hidden well.
From ashes rise the spirits bright,
In rebirth's dance, they claim their light.

With every breath, the cycle spins,
Death's gentle hand, where life begins.
A sacred oath we pledge anew,
The promise whispered, tried and true.

Through trials hard, the spirit's flight,
We learn to love, to shine our light.
Together woven, heart to heart,
In this lattice, we play our part.

So gather close, let love abide,
In every storm, we'll turn the tide.
A vow of faith, transformed and free,
In the lattice of eternity.

The Prophet's Journey

On winding roads the prophets tread,
With humble hearts, and souls widespread.
They seek the truth in tales of old,
A legacy of faith, unfold.

Through valleys dark and mountains high,
They carry hope, their spirits fly.
To every corner of the land,
With words of wisdom, they take a stand.

Their voices rise like morning dew,
In echoes vast, the message true.
With every step, the world they change,
In silent prayers, hearts rearrange.

From ancient scrolls, they draw their light,
A beacon bright, through darkest night.
To guide the lost, and heal the pain,
In unity, their souls remain.

So heed the call, embrace the quest,
For in this journey, we find our rest.
The prophet's path, though winding, vast,
Is paved with love, and shadows cast.

The Prayer of Rediscovery

In quiet moments, I seek Your grace,
Reviving my spirit in Your embrace.
Lost in the shadows, now I yearn,
To feel the warmth of Your love return.

With humbled heart, I raise my plea,
Guide my footsteps, Lord, set me free.
In every whisper, in every tear,
Let Your presence draw ever near.

The path of faith, though winding and steep,
Is illuminated by promises deep.
In the stillness, I find my way,
Through trials of night, to the dawn of day.

Awaken my soul, let it sing,
Of the wonders and joy You bring.
In Your wisdom, I find my quest,
To seek Your light and find my rest.

So I pray with fervor, without disguise,
Trusting Your plan, to lift me high.
In this journey, I will remain,
Faithful and true, through joy and pain.

Echoes of the Heart's Whisper

In the silence, I hear Your call,
An echo resounding, embracing all.
The heart's soft murmur, a sacred sound,
In Your love, my purpose is found.

Each breath is a song, a hymn in the night,
A testament to grace, a beacon of light.
In shadows where doubts may often confide,
Your truth remains ever my guide.

Through valleys of sorrow, I tread with hope,
In the folds of Your mercy, I learn to cope.
You cradle my fears, mend what is torn,
In the embrace of dawn, I am reborn.

With every heartbeat, I feel Your grace,
A dance of devotion, a sweet, holy place.
In love's gentle whisper, I find my way,
Trusting Your presence, come what may.

So here I stand, on faith's firm ground,
In Your eternal arms, security found.
Each echo of love resounds bright and clear,
Through the depths of my heart, You draw me near.

The Journey Back to the Divine

On a winding road, my heart begins,
To seek the light where love never ends.
Footsteps guided by faith's gentle hand,
In search of grace, through this holy land.

In moments of stillness, my spirit takes flight,
Awash in the glow of Your endless light.
Each challenge faced, a lesson profound,
In surrender and trust, Your peace is found.

With every prayer, I shed my despair,
Inviting Your joy, breathing in prayer.
Through trials endured, I learn to grow,
In the depths of my soul, Your love will flow.

As I journey back, the path unwinds,
Connecting my spirit to great designs.
With unwavering courage, I rise and stand,
Embraced by the heart of the Divine's hand.

So lead me, O Spirit, to shadows uncast,
Where whispers of wisdom hold steadfast.
Each step I take, in this sacred dance,
Leads me closer to love's true romance.

Chasing the Flicker of Light

In the stillness, a flicker ignites,
Drawing my soul to heavenly sights.
Each spark a promise, each glow a guide,
In the arms of Your love, I will abide.

Through valleys of doubt, I wander and roam,
In search of the light that leads me home.
With every heartbeat, the flame starts to rise,
Guided by faith beyond earthly ties.

In the chaotic world, I long to find,
The whispers of joy that soothe the mind.
Your light is a lantern, brightening the night,
Chasing shadows, infusing my fight.

Through trials I face, hope shines ever bright,
The flicker I follow, my spirit takes flight.
In the tapestry woven, my heart is replete,
With love that withstands all cycles, discreet.

As I chase the dawn, I find my place,
In the journey of life, in Your warm embrace.
With a flicker of faith, I'll rise and soar,
To the heights of Your love, forevermore.

In the Garden of Lost Dreams

Amidst the petals of forgotten time,
Whispers linger, softly divine.
In shadows where hopes gently sigh,
Faith blossoms beneath the sky.

With every tear that kisses the ground,
Miracles of grace can be found.
Nature's hymn, a sacred tune,
Awakens the heart, like the moon.

The thorns of doubt may pierce the soul,
Yet love's embrace can make us whole.
In the silence, sacred and near,
The garden blooms with hope sincere.

Beneath the arching branches wide,
Hearts gather in love, side by side.
Lost dreams rise like the morning dew,
In faith's embrace, we find what's true.

Rebirth in the Light of Faith

From ashes where the past once lay,
Hope emerges, bright as day.
In the warmth of love's embrace,
New beginnings find their place.

Each dawn the spirit starts anew,
With every breath, the heart breaks through.
In glimmers of celestial grace,
Divine light shines on every face.

The whispers of the heavens call,
Inviting us to rise and fall.
Through trials faced and sorrows borne,
We gather strength, reborn at dawn.

In faith's journey, we find our way,
A boundless love, brightening the gray.
Together we rise with faith in hand,
A community, forever we stand.

Unraveling the Divine Mysteries

In the depths of the quiet night,
Stars unveil their sacred light.
With each heartbeat, secrets unfurl,
Echoes of the divine swirl.

Through shadows, the answers weave,
In stillness, we learn to believe.
The tapestry of time and fate,
Whispers of love, both small and great.

In nature's cradle, we feel the flow,
A dance of spirits, ebb and glow.
Questions linger, yet faith remains,
In the heart, the divine explains.

As the universe stretches wide,
We ponder the sacred tide.
Unraveling mysteries with each prayer,
Embracing the presence everywhere.

Revelations in Silence

In silence, the truest words arise,
Echoes of the heart, wisdom wise.
The stillness holds what's meant to be,
A glimpse of eternity in me.

Each pause a doorway to the divine,
Where souls gather, perfectly aligned.
With every breath, a prayer takes flight,
Revelations dance in the soft twilight.

The quietude whispers secrets old,
In the hush, the spirit unfolds.
Confessions of the heart, sincere,
In silence, our purpose is clear.

Together we embrace the peace,
As chaos around us finds release.
In the depth of silence, we are found,
Revelations bloom, profound.

The Labyrinth of Purpose Revisited

In shadows cast by ancient trees,
We wander paths of whispered prayers.
Each step unfolds our mysteries,
In search of truth, the soul prepares.

With faith as guide through night's embrace,
We seek the light, the holy flame.
To journey on, we find our place,
In corridors of love's own name.

The heart, a compass built of trust,
Navigates through the maze of time.
Each turn we take, a path unjust,
Yet leads us to the love divine.

Among the echoes of the sage,
We learn that grace walks hand in hand.
In every chapter, every page,
Reveals the purpose, heaven planned.

Light shines anew in every pain,
Transforming tears to drops of gold.
Through labyrinths, we break the chain,
Our spirits rise, as fate unfolds.

Breath of the Seraphim

In silence deep, the whispers soar,
The breath of angels fills the air.
Each note, a hymn forevermore,
Awakens hope in earnest prayer.

They guide us through the darkened veil,
On wings of love, they carry dreams.
Through trials faced, we shall not fail,
For grace is stronger than it seems.

With every heartbeat, sacred sound,
The pulse of life, the joy of grace.
In unity, we shall be bound,
Within the light's warm, sweet embrace.

Let faith arise in every soul,
As seraphim fly high above.
Together, we will reach the goal,
And bask in endless, holy love.

In stillness, hear the call so pure,
The breath of heaven on our skin.
In every heart, a truth secure,
A promise shared, where love begins.

Reawakening in the Stillness

In quietude, the spirit brews,
A gentle stir in life's own heart.
Amidst the chaos, we will choose,
To find the peace that sets apart.

The morning light with hope arrives,
Illuminating paths of grace.
In stillness, we reclaim our lives,
Embracing love's tender embrace.

Each breath a prayer, a sweet release,
Finding in solitude our song.
The world may spin, yet we find peace,
In sacred moments, where we belong.

Awakened souls in tranquil tide,
We learn to dance in quiet bliss.
With hearts aligned and arms spread wide,
We greet the dawn, a sacred kiss.

In every heartbeat, whispers flow,
Reminding us of love's own grace.
In stillness found, our spirits grow,
Reawakening in love's embrace.

The Celestial Compass

The stars align in skies so bright,
A compass guiding through the night.
In every twinkle, wisdom glows,
As paths of destiny unfold.

With sacred light, our hearts ignite,
A journey blessed, a holy rite.
In every shadow, hope appears,
Unveiling truth through all our fears.

The winds of change, they softly blow,
Reminding us we're not alone.
With every breath, our spirits flow,
In harmony, we find our home.

Let faith be more than simply words,
But actions woven in the light.
The celestial dance of faithful herds,
Unites us all in love's pure sight.

In night's embrace, the compass turns,
Aligning with our truest call.
In every heart, a passion burns,
The journey's grace, embracing all.

The Star

In the night so dark and deep,
A glimmer shines, a promise keep.
Guiding hearts through trials faced,
A beacon bright, with love embraced.

From heavens high, it casts its light,
A whispered prayer, a sacred sight.
With every wish, it hears our call,
Uniting souls, inviting all.

In sorrow's gloom, it finds a way,
To lift our spirits, night to day.
The light of faith, it burns so clear,
Dispelling doubts, casting out fear.

O Star of hope, forever shine,
Your warmth, a gift, your love divine.
Through every storm, you lead us home,
In endless skies, where we can roam.

To distant lands and realms unknown,
With you beside, we are never alone.
A guiding force, a tranquil sea,
In thee we trust, eternally.

The Soul

In the heart's quiet, whispers dwell,
A sacred place, where love can swell.
A dance of spirit, pure and bright,
Awakening dreams, igniting light.

Through shadows cast, it finds its way,
In moments soft, where silence stays.
Each breath a song, a gentle tide,
The essence deep, where hopes abide.

Threads of the universe intertwine,
In every fiber, divine design.
With joy and sorrow, hand in hand,
The soul connects, a timeless band.

Unfurling wings on journeys vast,
In seeking truth, the die is cast.
Infinite paths that lead us near,
To sacred peace, beyond all fear.

O soul of mine, forever rise,
In unity with stars and skies.
The essence pure, our spirits soar,
In love's embrace, forevermore.

The Journey

Life's a road, winding and long,
With each step made, we grow strong.
Through valleys low and mountains high,
The spirit quests, it dares to fly.

In trials faced, we find our grace,
Each stumble leads to a new place.
With faith as guide, we forge ahead,
In shadows cast, new paths are spread.

The footprints left, a story told,
Of hearts entwined, of souls so bold.
In every tear, a lesson earned,
In every joy, a candle burned.

Through deserts wide, and oceans vast,
The journey teaches, we learn at last.
In moments still, we hear the call,
Of love that binds and lifts us all.

Embrace the road, wherever it leads,
For every heart knows its own needs.
In every ending, a brand new start,
The journey's sacred, a work of art.

The Song of the Inner Traveler

Deep within, a song does play,
A melody that leads the way.
The traveler's heart, a gentle guide,
Through echoes vast, it will abide.

In whispers soft, the spirit speaks,
In quiet dawns, where wisdom seeks.
With every note, a truth revealed,
In harmony, the soul is healed.

Through winding paths and starry nights,
The song resounds, igniting lights.
A chorus of dreams, a sacred sound,
In every heart, the song is found.

With every breath, we join the tune,
In joy and sorrow, under the moon.
The rhythm flows, like rivers wide,
A journey shared, where hearts collide.

O traveler bold, take flight on high,
With wings of faith, let spirits fly.
In every moment, the song will stay,
Forever echo, come what may.

Illuminated by Spirit

In stillness, we beseech the light,
Of grace bestowed, so pure and bright.
With open hearts, we seek the flame,
To guide us home, to share His name.

From shadows deep, the spirit calls,
In timeless truth, we rise and fall.
A whisper soft, a sacred breath,
Awakening souls to endless depth.

In unity, we find our way,
Each strand of faith, a bright array.
Together in this blessed place,
We mirror love, we show His grace.

With every prayer, the spirit flows,
In sacred circles, compassion grows.
We dance in joy, beneath the skies,
A symphony of hearts that rise.

In gratitude, we trust and sing,
Embracing all the love He brings.
With open hands, in faith we share,
This illuminated path we bear.

The Altar of Reflection

Before the altar, still I stand,
In quiet grace, I clasp Your hand.
Each thought a prayer, each breath a plea,
In humble awe, I long for Thee.

The echoes of my heart do speak,
In sacred silence, I feel weak.
Yet in this space, Your love abides,
A gentle tide, where hope resides.

Upon this altar, tears may flow,
Yet with each drop, new seeds I sow.
For in the pain, a vision grows,
A path of light, where mercy flows.

In whispers soft, You lead my way,
With every step, I choose to stay.
The altar speaks, my spirit soars,
In holy trust, my heart restores.

As shadows fade, my spirit shines,
In every crack, Your love entwines.
I find my place, my spirit free,
At the altar, Lord, I worship Thee.

Wandering in Spiritual Wilderness

In every forest, shadows dance,
I seek Your face, in every chance.
The wilderness, both wild and free,
A journey deep, to find my plea.

With every step, the earth does speak,
Through silent woods, the heart feels meek.
In rustling leaves, Your voice I hear,
Guiding my soul, dispelling fear.

The trials come, like storms that rage,
Yet in Your love, I turn the page.
Each lesson learned, a sacred gift,
In wilderness, my heart shall lift.

Through valleys low, and mountains high,
I'll raise my hands, to You I cry.
In every breath, Your essence found,
In wandering, my spirit's bound.

Wilderness, a sacred space,
Where lostness leads to found grace.
In solitude, my heart will sing,
In every wandering, You are King.

The Invitation to the Sacred Dance

Come, take my hand, and let us sway,
In sacred rhythm, night and day.
The dance of life, so wild, so true,
Together, Lord, we'll move anew.

In every step, we find our song,
With every beat, we all belong.
A circle wide, where spirits meet,
In unity, our hearts do greet.

The alleluias lift the air,
In joyful leaps, we lose our care.
Your light illuminates the floor,
As we embrace forevermore.

Through trials faced, we twirl and spin,
In sacred trust, we rise within.
With every turn, Your love revealed,
In this bright dance, our wounds are healed.

So join the dance, O hearts divine,
As Heaven sings, and stars align.
In sacred movement, free and grand,
We twirl as one, held by His hand.

Unraveling Sacred Threads

In the quiet morn, whispers rise,
Threads of faith weave through the sky.
Hearts entwined with sacred song,
Souls awakening where they belong.

Each prayer a stitch, a gentle tie,
Binding us near, as spirits fly.
In the tapestry, colors blend,
Crafting the stories our journeys send.

With every tear, a lesson learned,
In trials faced, our spirits burned.
The loom of love, our hands embrace,
In sacred threads, we find our place.

Under the stars, we gather forth,
Sharing our tales of joy and worth.
Among the shadows, light will break,
Unraveling truth for love's own sake.

Together we rise, a chorus bright,
Lost in the rhythm, transformed by light.
In unity's grace, each heart a guide,
Through sacred threads, we turn the tide.

The Altar of Self-Discovery

Upon the altar, mirrors gleam,
Reflections dance in sacred dreams.
Here, the soul seeks, silent and still,
To uncover the depths of its will.

A flame ignites from truth unveiled,
The heart once bound now has sailed.
Each breath a prayer, a step anew,
In the embrace of skies so blue.

Beneath the weight of past despair,
Hope springs forth in tender care.
With every choice, the spirit sings,
The altar holds what freedom brings.

In solitude's grace, we find our way,
The whispers of purpose guide each day.
A journey inward, profound and vast,
Unlocking treasures of the past.

We rise from shadows, a phoenix bold,
The altar's gifts, pure love foretold.
In self-discovery, hearts intertwine,
Seeking the divine in love's own line.

Transcendence of the Weary Heart

When burdens weigh and shadows loom,
The weary heart begins to bloom.
In desperate night, hope finds a spark,
Transcending pain, igniting the dark.

Through trials faced, the spirit grows,
In the struggle, true strength shows.
With every tear, the soul expands,
Transcending fear with faith's gentle hands.

In silence deep, the heart does speak,
A melody of love so unique.
With every heartbeat, a soft refrain,
Transcendence found in joy and pain.

The light shines bright within the soul,
In the journey's weave, we find our role.
Embracing the weary with open arms,
Transcending sorrow, love's healing charms.

Together we rise, renewed and whole,
The weary heart, reborn, consoled.
In unity's bond, we take our part,
Attaining peace, the weary heart.

Beneath Heaven's Gaze

Beneath heaven's gaze, a prayer unspooled,
In the stillness, the heart is ruled.
Each star a witness, each sigh a sign,
In this sacred moment, souls align.

With outstretched hands, we seek the grace,
Embracing the love in this holy space.
Within the quiet, whispers embrace,
Beneath heaven's gaze, we find our place.

In nature's arms, the spirit flows,
The dance of life in all that grows.
Each breath a hymn, a sacred tune,
Under the watchful eye of the moon.

Here faith awakens, doubts take flight,
As hearts unite, the world feels right.
Beneath heaven's gaze, souls entwine,
Transcending the limits of space and time.

With gratitude deep, we lift our eyes,
Experiencing truth in the boundless skies.
In every heartbeat, a echo of praise,
Beneath heaven's gaze, in love ablaze.

Embracing the Pilgrim's Soul

In every step, the heart does seek,
A path where faith and hope do speak.
The road is long, yet grace will guide,
Through valleys low, and mountains wide.

With every breath, the spirit's flight,
A whisper soft in the starry night.
The pilgrim walks with burdens light,
For wisdom shines like morning light.

Where shadows cast, the light shall break,
In moments deep, our souls awake.
Each trial faced, a chance to grow,
In surrender sweet, His love we know.

In unity, the hearts align,
The sacred bond, the love divine.
We gather strength, our voices raise,
In gratitude, we sing His praise.

Embrace the journey, trust the call,
For every rise, you'll never fall.
The pilgrim's way, a path so true,
In every step, He walks with you.

Surrendering to the Infinite

In silent prayer, we find our peace,
Where doubts subside and worries cease.
We cast our fears to winds so free,
In surrendering, we truly see.

The vast expanse, His love does fill,
In every challenge, He gives us will.
Trust is the anchor in stormy seas,
In stillness, hearts begin to ease.

Let go the weight that binds the soul,
In gentle hands, we find our whole.
With open hearts, we seek the light,
In shadows dark, He shines so bright.

To rise above, our spirits soar,
In unity, we seek for more.
The infinite beckons, sweet and clear,
In every heartbeat, His presence near.

Embrace the vastness, let love flow,
In every heartbeat, let faith grow.
In surrendering, we find our way,
To the sacred promise of each day.

The Echo of a Higher Calling

A whisper calls, through dreams it weaves,
Awakening hope, beneath the leaves.
In every heart, a truth unfolds,
A story deep, in silence told.

With gentle nudges, life invites,
To step beyond the darkest nights.
Each breath a gift, each moment pure,
In love's embrace, we feel secure.

The echoes ring, of lives well-lived,
A tapestry of grace we give.
Through trials faced, and joys we share,
In unity, we rise, aware.

Listen closely, the call is clear,
It sings of love, it conquers fear.
The heart knows truth, it won't delay,
In every echo, find the way.

Awake your spirit, let it sing,
For higher calling, hope does bring.
Embrace the light, let shadows fall,
In every heart, we heed the call.

Beneath the Surface of Chaos

In chaos loud, the heart beats strong,
A rhythm lost, yet still belongs.
Beneath the storms, a calm we find,
Within the chaos, peace aligned.

In swirling winds, the soul does yearn,
For love that guides, a heart can learn.
With every tempest, we learn to rise,
In the silent depths, faith never dies.

The world may rush, yet we stand still,
In every moment, trust His will.
For in the chaos, we are reborn,
In whispers sweet, the dawn is sworn.

Beneath the surface, beauty grows,
In hidden places, love bestows.
In storms we weather, find our grace,
In every trial, we seek His face.

So hold your heart, let chaos flow,
In depths of love, our spirits glow.
For beneath the waves, the truth will shine,
In every heartbeat, we are divine.

Beneath the Weight of Faith

In shadows deep, the heart will strain,
Yet in the night, the light remains.
With every tear, a seed is sown,
For in our trials, we are not alone.

Hands raised high, in fervent prayer,
A whisper's grace, we feel it there.
In trust we walk, though paths be rough,
Our spirits soar, our souls are tough.

The weight of doubt, it clings like night,
But faith shall guide, a beacon bright.
Through tempests fierce, we find our way,
For in His love, we choose to stay.

Each burden borne, a chance to grow,
Through valleys low, our spirits flow.
In fellowship, we gather round,
A strength in numbers, faith profound.

So let us tread, with hearts aflame,
In unity, we call His name.
For every struggle, every fight,
Beneath our faith, we find our light.

The Mirror of the Ancients

In ancient texts, the wisdom flows,
Reflections true that time bestows.
With every word, a story told,
A glimpse of truth, both brave and bold.

Beneath the stars, the sages speak,
Their voices strong, the lost we seek.
In sacred words, our lives entwined,
A tapestry of the divine.

The ages past, they guide our way,
In silent prayers, we choose to stay.
With every page, a lesson learned,
In echoes deep, our spirits yearned.

Through trials faced by those before,
We stand on faith, forevermore.
In courage found, we forge ahead,
Our hearts ablaze, by love we're led.

In every heart, the echoes ring,
Of ancient souls, their spirits sing.
In unity, we rise as one,
With every dawn, a new day begun.

So let us seek the mirrored light,
In ancient paths, our future bright.
For in their wisdom, we are shown,
The strength of love, we've always known.

Embracing the Quietude

In silence deep, the spirit grows,
A sacred space, where peace bestows.
With every breath, the stillness calls,
In quietude, our spirit enthralls.

The world may rush, but here we stand,
In whispered prayers, we join His hand.
Amidst the storm, we find our grace,
In gentle moments, we seek His face.

Each heartbeat soft, a rhythmic flow,
In tranquil thoughts, our spirits glow.
We gather strength from silence sweet,
In quietude, our hearts repeat.

Let distractions fade, let worries cease,
In stillness found, we find our peace.
For in that calm, we hear Him speak,
In every pause, our souls grow meek.

So hold the silence, hold it tight,
Embrace the dawn, embrace the light.
For in our hearts, the truth shall dwell,
In quietude, all will be well.

Divine Echoes of the Past

In the echoes of the past, we find,
The threads of grace that intertwine.
Through ages gone, their voices soar,
In timeless rhymes, our spirits explore.

The lessons learned, in shadows cast,
A guiding light, foreverlast.
In whispered tales, we shape our fate,
With every story, we elevate.

From ancient dawns, their truths abide,
In sacred texts, our hearts reside.
Through trials faced and dreams pursued,
The echoes ring, our souls renewed.

A symphony of lives lived well,
Through every trial, their spirits swell.
In every strength, an echo clear,
Reminding us that God is near.

So let us walk, with heads held high,
With every step, we touch the sky.
For in the past, we hear the call,
The divine echoes unite us all.

The Ritual of Return

In silence we gather, hearts open wide,
Seeking the path where the ancients reside.
With whispered prayers, we call on the day,
A journey begun, in faith, we shall stay.

Through shadows we wander, illuminated dreams,
Guided by visions and celestial beams.
Each step a reminder, each breath a sigh,
The spirit awakens, the past draws nigh.

In sacred circles, we share our truth,
With hearts entwined, we reclaim our youth.
The echoes of wisdom, in harmony ring,
As echoes of gratitude rise and take wing.

We cleanse in the waters, the river of grace,
Reflecting the laughter upon every face.
With each gentle wave, our burdens release,
In the ritual of return, we find our peace.

Together we celebrate, united in song,
In the dance of creation, where all belong.
The past and the future, entwined as one,
In the heart of the journey, our souls are spun.

Pilgrimage through the Soul's Forest

In the depths of the forest, where shadows grow deep,
The whispers of ancients in silence do seep.
With each step I take, on this sacred ground,
I seek the lost wisdom, where truth can be found.

The trees stand as witnesses, silent and tall,
Their branches like arms, they cradle us all.
With roots that are tangled, our stories combine,
In the pilgrimage deep, we search for the divine.

Through the rustling leaves, the spirits do call,
In the echoes of nature, we feel the enthrall.
The light filters through, as dawn paints the sky,
In the soul's gentle forest, we learn how to fly.

With each breath I take, I inhale the peace,
In this sacred sanctuary, my worries release.
The wisdom of nature wraps round like a shawl,
As I walk through the forest, I answer the call.

Emerging from shadows, reborn and renewed,
I carry the blessings, the light I imbued.
With every step forward, my heart now believes,
In the pilgrimage sought, the soul ever cleaves.

The Light of a Thousand Stars

In the night sky above, a canvas of dreams,
The light of a thousand stars brightly redeems.
Guiding our journey, each twinkle, a prayer,
In the vastness of darkness, we find hope to share.

The cosmos, a testament, ancient and wise,
Each star, a reminder, beneath infinite skies.
With hearts full of wonder, we gaze and we yearn,
For the lessons of love that the heavens return.

With every star shining, a story unfolds,
Of paths that were taken, of destinies bold.
In the dance of the galaxies, truths intertwine,
As we open our hearts, the universe signs.

In unity gathered, together we rise,
Creating our wishes, like stars in the skies.
The light is our guide, through the shadows we face,
With the love of our spirits, we journey through space.

Embracing the night, with all its embrace,
In the light of those stars, we find our true place.
Forever we wander, through time and through space,
In the heart of the cosmos, we find our grace.

Journeying to the Heart of Wholeness

In the stillness of being, we wander within,
The heart of our essence, where silence begins.
With each gentle heartbeat, a rhythm of grace,
We journey together, no need to chase.

The mountains of wisdom, the rivers of peace,
Each moment a blessing, each fragment a piece.
The path to the heart is a spiral of light,
Illuminating shadows, transforming the night.

In the gathering circle, we're joined hand in hand,
We carry the stories of every land.
With voices united, in harmony ring,
A symphony sacred, our spirits take wing.

With courage we step, into the unknown,
In the heart of our journey, we're never alone.
Each trial a teacher, each joy a reward,
In the dance of the cosmos, our spirits are soared.

To the heart of wholeness, we journey and grow,
In the embrace of the universe, love's gentle flow.
Through laughter and sorrow, we strengthen our ties,
In the journey together, our spirits shall rise.

The Song of Reclamation

In the quiet dawn, a hush unfolds,
Voices rising, like tales of old.
Hope whispers softly, in the morning mist,
Hearts entwined in an eternal tryst.

With every step, the earth awakes,
A dance of souls, no heart forsakes.
In unity we gather, hand in hand,
Reclaiming the promise of this sacred land.

The rivers flow with stories anew,
Each drop a prayer, each wave a cue.
The mountains echo with ancient grace,
Resilience shines upon every face.

The sun sets low, painting skies aglow,
In shadows cast, our spirits grow.
Together we rise, to claim what's ours,
In the night's embrace, we find our stars.

The circle whole, the voices strong,
In every heartbeat, we sing our song.
Through trials faced, we stand as one,
In the song of reclamation, we have won.

A Testament of the Sought

In the wilderness, the seekers roam,
Each step a journey, far from home.
With open hearts, we sift through pain,
In whispers soft, our souls regain.

The sky above, a canvas vast,
Painting dreams of the shadowed past.
We plead for guidance, through the night,
A testament shines, a flickering light.

In silent prayers, the truth is found,
Among the lost, where hope is crowned.
We share the burdens, burdens shared,
In every moment, we are spared.

The sacred speaks through every tear,
Transforming trials into steadfast cheer.
In solitude, we learn to trust,
A testament unfolds, it's a must.

So gather close, the chains must break,
In unity's embrace, the vow we make.
For in the journey, the sought we see,
A testament of love will set us free.

Resurrecting the Sacred Flame

In the darkness, a flicker glows,
From ashes cooled, the spirit flows.
With tender hands, we breathe anew,
Resurrecting hope, in love's sweet view.

The sacred flame, it dances bright,
Illuminating hearts, banishing night.
With every ember, stories rise,
A sacred song beneath the skies.

Together we gather, the circle drawn,
In the warmth of the flame, fear is gone.
Through sacred rites, the past restored,
Resurrecting life in every chord.

With voices lifted, we cast our prayer,
Each note a promise, a breath of air.
In the sacred space, we find our claim,
Resurrecting the love, igniting the flame.

The world transforms with every song,
In the heart's embrace, we all belong.
From ashes born, our spirits soar,
Resurrecting the sacred flame, forevermore.

Awakening the Spirit Within

In the stillness, a whisper calls,
Awakening echoes through ancient halls.
The spirit stirs, in silence profound,
In every heartbeat, the truth is found.

With gentle grace, the journey starts,
Uniting fragments of shattered parts.
In labyrinth paths, we seek the light,
Awakening souls, igniting the night.

From shadows deep, we emerge whole,
Awakening purpose in each soul.
Transcending doubt, we learn to trust,
In the depths of being, we find what's just.

With open eyes, the vision clear,
Awakening whispers, drawing near.
In the tapestry of fate, we weave,
A spirit reclaimed, in love believe.

Together we rise, as one we shine,
Awakening truth in the sacred line.
With every breath, the journey flows,
The spirit within, forever glows.

The Throne of Inner Truth

In the silence where whispers dwell,
The heart knows secrets it cannot tell.
With faith as light, it guides the way,
To the throne where true spirits stay.

Beneath the crowns, shadows softly fall,
Calling us to rise, answering the call.
In the stillness, wisdom unfolds,
A story of freedom, waiting to be told.

Veils of doubt may cloud our sight,
Yet truth shines forth, an eternal light.
Amidst the chaos, we seek to find,
The sanctity of soul intertwined.

Each tear shed is a prayer released,
A melody of pain that seeks its peace.
In the heart's chamber, love wakes the soul,
Inviting us home, to be once whole.

Rising from ashes, our spirits soar,
Embracing the path that leads to restore.
In sacred spaces, we kneel and bow,
To the essence of truth, our holy vow.

Chords of the Heart's Lament

In shadows thick where sorrows dwell,
The heart strings tremble, a sacred bell.
Every note, a whisper of pain,
Resonating love, through joy and rain.

Melodies linger, in twilight's grace,
Echoes of past that time can't erase.
In the stillness, the soul does weep,
Holding the dreams that once dared to leap.

Here in the silence, visions collide,
A journey of loss, with love as our guide.
Strumming the chords of a heart once bright,
Finding the way back to sacred light.

For in the lament, renewal is found,
A dance of the heart in divine surround.
With each gentle sigh, we open wide,
The doors of grace where hope will abide.

Though shadows may linger, and fears might rise,
Together we stand, under vast, open skies.
Transcending the sorrow, in truth we unite,
Singing the hymn of eternal light.

Reclaiming the Sacred Path

Down the winding trails we tread,
With faith as our guide, the light ahead.
In whispers of wind, the ancients call,
Reclaiming the path, where we stand tall.

With every step, the earth does sing,
Of stories forgotten, of hope in spring.
From shadows we've risen, now visibly free,
Embracing the sacred, as it shall be.

Footprints of past in soil remain,
Telling of trials, of joy and pain.
Yet forward we move, hearts intertwined,
With love as our compass, we seek and find.

In the spaces where spirit ignites,
We unearth the truth that softly invites.
A promise of grace, in each fleeting breath,
Reclaiming the sacred, defying death.

Together we walk, hands clasped in peace,
Our souls ablaze, may the journey not cease.
In the dawn's embrace, we rise and proclaim,
The sacred path leads us home again.

The Bridge to Inner Peace

In the quiet waters where stillness reigns,
A bridge emerges, where love sustains.
Crossing the currents, we find our way,
To the heart of stillness where shadows sway.

Through valleys of doubt, we seek to roam,
Yet peace whispers softly, 'You are home.'
In the embrace of calm, fears fade away,
Guiding our journey to an eternal day.

Each step on the bridge, a prayer fulfilled,
Unity blossoms, our hearts be thrilled.
In the dawn's light, we gather our grace,
Finding our solace in this sacred space.

With the rhythm of breath, we enter the truth,
The bridge becomes stronger, embracing our youth.
In the flow of being, we understand,
Inner peace awaits, a sacred demand.

As we traverse the expanse of love,
The bridge takes us higher, with help from above.
In the stillness and calm, we rise, we release,
Finding our way on the bridge to peace.

A Journey Through Sacred Time

In stillness, we wander the path so bright,
Guided by whispers of ancient light.
Each step a prayer, each moment a sign,
Time's sacred dance, our hearts entwine.

Through valleys of doubt, we silently roam,
In trials, we find the seeds of our home.
The mountains echo the stories of old,
As courage blooms in the hearts of the bold.

With every sunrise, a promise we greet,
In the tapestry woven, our lives are complete.
The sacredness shines through the shadows and tears,
In love's warm embrace, we'll conquer our fears.

As seasons change and the rivers flow,
We learn to trust in the ebb and the glow.
Footprints in sand, they wash with the tide,
Yet faith anchors deep, forever our guide.

In unity found, our spirits take flight,
Together we journey, through day and night.
In the ending's embrace, new beginnings arise,
A journey through time, beneath endless skies.

Illuminated by Grace

In shadows of longing, where hope seems to fade,
A light shines within, by grace we are swayed.
With hearts open wide, we seek the divine,
Illuminated whispers, in stillness we find.

Like stars in the heavens, each soul has its glow,
In compassion's embrace, our spirits will grow.
Through trials and triumphs, together we rise,
Benedictions of light, beneath endless skies.

In the quiet moments, when doubts start to creep,
Love's gentle whisper calls us from sleep.
Faith dances lightly, on winds of the soul,
Illuminating paths, making broken hearts whole.

Each trial a blessing, each tear a reset,
In grace, we find strength in times we forget.
With love as our compass, in unity we stand,
Navigating life, holding faith in our hands.

In gratitude's song, we find our true place,
All beings connected, wrapped in love's grace.
Let us walk together, through joy and despair,
Illuminated by grace, with love as our prayer.

The Testament of the Soul

In the still of the night, our spirits take flight,
Whispers of wisdom, in shadows, they write.
Each breath a testament, each heartbeat a call,
To seek and discover the truths of it all.

With words unspoken, our souls intertwine,
In the tapestry woven, a design so divine.
We rise and we stumble, we dance in the rain,
The testament flows through joy and through pain.

In moments of silence, our essence is bare,
Reflecting the light that resides everywhere.
Through valleys and peaks, we journey as one,
The testament whispers, we're never undone.

With faith as our anchor and love as our guide,
We move through the world, with hearts opened wide.
Each chapter revealing the story we write,
The testament of the soul shines ever so bright.

In the embrace of the divine, we discover our goal,
To live as a promise, the testament of the soul.
With every connection, the universe sings,
In unity found, the joy that it brings.

Kindling the Flame of Faith

In the heart of the night, a flicker appears,
A spark of belief, dispelling our fears.
With courage ignited, we rise from the damp,
Kindling the flame, a warm guiding lamp.

For every dark moment, a reason to stand,
In faith's gentle glow, we'll lend a hand.
Through valleys of doubt, through mountains of pain,
We find hope in the fire, our love will remain.

Each breath is a whisper, a promise in time,
The strength of the spirit, a rhythm, a rhyme.
With hearts intertwined, we dance through the storm,
Kindling the flame of faith keeps us warm.

In unity's power, together we weave,
A tapestry bright, in which we believe.
Through trials and triumphs, we rise from the ash,
The flame of our faith is a brilliant splash.

Let hope be the fuel that drives us each day,
In the circle of life, we find our own way.
With love as our anchor, forever we'll stay,
Kindling the flame of faith, come what may.

The Path of Self-Discovery

In silence I wander, seeking the light,
My heart open wide, to truths in the night.
Each step that I take, reveals hidden way,
For deep in my soul, the answers will stay.

The whispers of ages, they guide me along,
Lessons of patience, of love, and of strong.
Within I find strength, through trials I face,
Each challenge a gift, beneath Heaven's grace.

The mirror reflects, my spirit so pure,
A journey of faith, in love I endure.
With every dawn's rise, a chance to renew,
On this sacred path, I find what is true.

Embracing the shadows, I learn to let go,
For wisdom is birthed, when ego's laid low.
In quiet repose, I meet my own gaze,
The depths of my soul, in the light I praise.

At the end of the road, I stand with a smile,
For every lost moment, has been worth the while.
In finding myself, I've learned to forgive,
The path of self-discovery, teaches us to live.

Beneath the Halo of Grace

Beneath the bright halo, of love and of peace,
I find in the stillness, my burdens release.
The embrace of the Spirit, tender and warm,
Guides my weary heart, away from the storm.

With each whispered prayer, I draw ever near,
To the source of my strength, casting out fear.
In moments of doubt, I recall this bright light,
Reminding me softly, that I am the right.

In shadows of anguish, a whisper I hear,
A promise of hope, dispelling my fear.
Each tear that I shed, turned into a song,
As love weaves its way, teaching me to be strong.

The warmth of divinity, shines ever so bright,
In the depth of my soul, igniting the night.
With faith as my anchor, I rise and I soar,
Beneath the halo, I am evermore.

In the canvas of life, grace paints every hue,
A vibrant tapestry, forever anew.
In gratitude's embrace, I humbly rejoice,
Beneath the halo of grace, I find my voice.

A Pilgrim's Return to Sacredness

In the hush of the dawn, a pilgrim I stand,
Walking the path, hand in hand with the Land.
My heart beats like drums, in the rhythm of prayer,
Each step a return, to the wisdom laid bare.

Through valleys of shadows, up mountains of light,
The journey unveils, what's hidden from sight.
With sacred intentions, I seek and I find,
The echoes of ages, entwining my mind.

In temples of nature, I breathe with the trees,
The whispers of spirit, like sweet summer breeze.
Each petal that falls, carries stories of old,
Like a treasure unwrapped, waiting to be told.

As I walk on this path, in reverence and grace,
I rekindle the flame, in each sacred space.
A pilgrim's return, a circle complete,
Embracing my truth, with each heartbeat's beat.

With faith as my compass, I follow the light,
In the tapestry woven, everything feels right.
Each breath is a blessing, revealing the way,
A pilgrim's return, to sacredness' sway.

The Soul's Mirror

In the quiet of night, I gaze in the glass,
A reflection of truth, as the moments pass.
The soul shows its colors, a spectrum so wide,
In the stillness I find, the love stored inside.

Each flaw, each virtue, a message so clear,
In shadows and light, I learn to draw near.
The mirror of soul, reveals what I hide,
With compassion and grace, in love I confide.

In the depths of this glance, my essence unfolds,
Stories of courage, and fears to be told.
With each sacred look, I embrace what I see,
The beauty of being, simply to be free.

As the dawn breaks anew, I cherish the glow,
Of the lessons learned, in the ebb and the flow.
Through the trials of life, in faith I will stand,
The soul's mirror shines, when I open my hand.

In moments of doubt, I find wisdom abide,
With love as my guide, and my heart open wide.
The soul's mirror reflects, what's pure and profound,
In the dance of existence, true peace can be found.

Harbingers of Inner Light

In the stillness, whispers rise,
Guiding souls to the skies.
Faith ignites a sacred flame,
Illuminating in His name.

Through trials steep, the spirit grows,
Love and mercy freely flow.
In each heart, a beacon shines,
Drawing forth the divine signs.

Hope awakens in the night,
A dance of shadows turns to light.
With each prayer, a pathway clears,
Wiping away the silent fears.

Let us gather, hearts in grace,
Together we shall find our place.
In the garden of the soul,
The spirit's song will make us whole.

With every step, our spirits soar,
Harbingers knock upon the door.
Enter in, let love ignite,
Bathed in the glow of inner light.

The Well of Resilience

In shadows deep, we seek the well,
Where weary hearts can dwell.
Cleansing waters, pure and bright,
In every drop, a spark of light.

Beneath the weight of bitter tears,
Strength emerges, calming fears.
With courage drawn from sacred springs,
The heart, renewed, with vigor sings.

Let trials come, unyielding waves,
For we are forged in sacred caves.
With each challenge, a lesson taught,
In resilience, the battles fought.

With love and grace, we rise once more,
Life's currents cannot shake our core.
From the depths, we find our song,
A melody where we belong.

The well runs deep, invite the light,
Fill our spirits, end the night.
Beneath the surface, peace abides,
In this well, our hope resides.

Gazing into the Infinite

With open hearts, we seek the vast,
Where time and space unite at last.
In the cosmos, whispers call,
In quiet moments, we find our all.

Stars dance brightly, stories twine,
In every twinkle, a sacred sign.
As we gaze into the unknown,
We feel the seeds of faith have grown.

Eternal questions linger near,
Echoing softly in our ear.
With each breath, we touch the sky,
In the infinite, we learn to fly.

Boundless love in every glance,
In the universe, we find our chance.
Gazing deep, our souls unite,
In stardust dreams, we find the light.

Throughout the night, our spirits rise,
To dance among celestial ties.
As we explore the sacred stream,
In the infinite, we dare to dream.

Celestial Answers Found

In quiet prayers, we lift our plea,
Seeking guidance, show us the way.
Amidst the chaos, voices clear,
Whispering truths we long to hear.

Celestial realms, a beacon bright,
Illuminating through the night.
In the silence, answers bloom,
Guiding hearts away from gloom.

With every heartbeat, divinity speaks,
In our struggles, hope it seeks.
Trust the journey, trust the sign,
In each moment, the divine aligns.

Let go of doubt, embrace the flow,
In faith's embrace, our spirits grow.
Celestial wisdom lights the way,
Transforming night into the day.

In unity, we find the grace,
With every step, we touch His face.
Celestial answers, near and far,
Guide our souls like a shining star.

A Dance with the Divine

In quiet moments, I shall sway,
With the light that guides my way,
In whispers soft, the Spirit calls,
In sacred halls, my spirit sprawls.

Each step a prayer, a heart's embrace,
In rhythm with the boundless grace,
The stars above, they twinkle bright,
A cosmic dance in the still of night.

Embracing love, both near and far,
With faith that glows like a guiding star,
In every twirl, I find my peace,
In every beat, my doubts release.

The music swells, a holy sound,
In sacred space, my soul is found,
As I ascend, the veil I lift,
In divine love, I find my gift.

So let my heart unite and flow,
In this sweet dance, my spirit grows,
In the arms of grace, I shall abide,
Together with the Divine, our souls collide.

The Well of Inner Peace

In the stillness of the dawn,
A whisper soft, a gentle yawn,
The waters calm, the surface clear,
I find my heart, I hold it dear.

With every drop, my worries fade,
In silent depths, my fears unmade,
The flowing stream does gently sigh,
A sacred place where I can fly.

Let go, release, the burdens weighed,
In this still well, I am remade,
The echoing truth, it softly calls,
Within my soul, the silence thralls.

Each moment spent, a breath divine,
In sacred stillness, I align,
Beneath the surface, joy unfurls,
In the depths of peace, my spirit twirls.

In humble grace, I drink my fill,
Deep in the well, my heart is still,
With every drop, the world recedes,
In inner peace, my spirit feeds.

Beneath Layers of Dust

In ancient scrolls, the truth lies bare,
Beneath the dust, a longing stare,
With each layer, a story told,
Of love, of hope, of hearts of gold.

In moments lost, the wisdom sleeps,
Awake, arise, for the soul it keeps,
With gentle hands, I brush away,
To find the light of yesterday.

History whispers, secrets spill,
In the quiet, a sacred thrill,
I seek the echoes of the past,
In every word, a shadow cast.

As I uncover, I feel the spark,
In every page, a sacred arc,
For buried deep, the spirit yearns,
In layers thin, the candle burns.

So let me wander, let me seek,
Beneath the dust, the spirit speaks,
A timeless hymn, a path of grace,
In uncovering, I find my place.

The Wings of Awakening

In quiet moments, wings take flight,
In the dawn's embrace, in morning light,
With every breath, my spirit soars,
Into the skies, where freedom roars.

The shadows fade, my heart ignites,
A journey vast, with sacred sights,
In every flutter, a chance to grow,
In awakening, my spirit glows.

With trust beneath, I rise above,
In every challenge, find pure love,
The winds of change, they guide my way,
In this ascent, I choose to stay.

Each feathered touch, a prayer ascends,
In the light of grace, my soul transcends,
To heights unknown, my heart can dream,
In the wings of hope, I find my theme.

So let me soar, on currents wide,
In the arms of love, I shall abide,
With wings of light, forever free,
In awakening, I find the key.

Voices of the Ancients

In whispers carried by the breeze,
The ancients speak through rustling leaves.
Their wisdom dances on the air,
Reminding us of sacred care.

Through shadows long and ages deep,
Their echoes in our hearts do seep.
With every dawn, their stories shine,
A link between the vast divine.

From mountain heights to ocean's roam,
They guide our souls, they lead us home.
In silence deep, their truths unfold,
A tapestry of grace retold.

So tread with love the paths they paved,
In ancient wisdom, we are saved.
Their voices hum a sacred song,
A hymn of hope that lingers long.

Let us embrace their gentle call,
For in their light, we rise, not fall.
Through ages past, their spirits thrive,
In every heart, their flames alive.

Rediscovering the Sacred Name

In quiet places, the name we seek,
A whisper soft, yet strong and unique.
With every breath, we chant in grace,
Finding solace in this sacred space.

The letters dance upon the tongue,
A melody of hope, forever sung.
In prayerful thought, our hearts entwine,
Rediscovering the sacred line.

Each syllable a spark divine,
Illuminating paths we find.
With open hearts, we seek the light,
In name revered, our souls take flight.

So let us gather, hand in hand,
In unity, together we stand.
With reverence, we call the name,
Across the world, it burns like flame.

As dawn breaks forth, our spirits rise,
In sacred sound, we touch the skies.
With every breath, we'll hold it dear,
The sacred name, forever near.

The Wisdom of Still Waters

In stillness deep, the waters flow,
Reflecting truth we long to know.
As surface calm conceals the depth,
In silence lies our heart's true breath.

Beneath the tides, the currents churn,
In quietude, we cease to yearn.
The mirror holds the light of stars,
A wisdom boundless, free from scars.

From ancient shores to rivers wide,
The waters speak, our faithful guide.
They share the secrets of the night,
Awakening the inner light.

So gather close and cast your fears,
Let go of doubt, embrace the years.
In gentle waves, your truth will rise,
The wisdom found in stillness lies.

With hearts attuned to waters' song,
We'll find the place where we belong.
In every ripple, peace will flow,
In still waters, our spirits grow.

Embracing the Eternal Within

In every heart, a spark resides,
A flame of love that never hides.
To find it, look beyond the veil,
Embrace the truth, let spirit sail.

Through trials faced and joys received,
In every moment, love believed.
The eternal whispers, soft and clear,
A gentle call that draws us near.

With open arms, we welcome grace,
In every shadow, we'll find our place.
The essence pure, the light that shines,
In unity, our heart aligns.

So dance through life with hearts ajar,
Recognizing just who you are.
Embracing love, our spirits soar,
In the eternal, forevermore.

In sacred silence, truth resides,
With every breath, the soul abides.
Embrace the light, let ego fall,
The eternal within, our all in all.

Milton Keynes UK
Ingram Content Group UK Ltd.
UKHW031320271124
451618UK00007B/200

9 789916 898352